INTRODUCTION

I was born a first class citizen. I entered into contracts that, without my knowledge, made me a second class citizen. I am working on the legal process of restoring my first class citizenship status.

I was surprised to find that the United States government recognized two distinct classes of citizens, let alone that my citizenship status had changed. At first I did not believe it. It was not Until I learned how to use the law library in the county court house that I was able to confirm my status. I am not an attorney so this book should not be considered as legal advice. It may be used for the basis of your own research. This book does not have a copyright, so you can copy all or part of it. This book borrows research from other books without copyrights written by people across the nation. I will describe the big picture first, then I will substantiate the claims made and give a more detailed picture later.

You may find the ideas presented here conflict with the model of government that you have been taught. You may also find these ideas impossible to believe. This is understandable. The further you read, the more you may change the way you filter information about what the government is doing. If you cannot believe any of this, please set this book aside. Sometime in the future, you may come back to this book and it may make more sense. I believe that the concepts described here are true. But, you should not! If you accepted the ideas in this book without confirming them from other sources, then you are a fool! If I can change your model of reality in one book then someone else might be able to fill your head with nonsense. Please be skeptical. Even if you do not agree with the central premise, you may agree with some of the research. If so, you will still get something out of this book. There are many Citizens doing research on the topics described in this book. Some will sell the results of their research while others will practically give it away. This book does not discuss some of the more advanced topics (Citizen militia, commercial liens, common law liens, common law trusts). At the end of this book, I will supply you with the names of books, magazines, newspapers, computer bulletin boards that fill in some of the details that I have excluded.

The Big Picture

The United States of America is a unique nation. It was the first constitutional republic in the world. Before the American Revolution, the King of England owned all the land in his colonies. The inhabitants of the colonies were his subjects. When the war was over, the King signed the Treaty of Peace. In that treaty he said that all the land in the former colonies was owned by the people and all of his sovereign powers that he held in the colonies were transferred, not to the government of the colonies but, to the People of the colonies. This made all of the Citizens of the colonies sovereigns. This has never happened before or since in any other country. In other countries, the government is sovereign. It makes laws for its subject-citizens and it gives them their rights. In the United States, the People were sovereigns. The People were endowed, by their creator, with certain rights and the government was instituted to secure those rights. We the People, gave a portion of our sovereignty to the state government, and the states gave a small portion of the sovereignty we gave to them, to the federal government so that it would be strong enough to defend the People. The Constitution for the United States of America describes the powers that the states gave to the federal government.

If the federal government is defined by the Constitution, and the Constitution says that I am a sovereign, why do I feel like a subject? I own my house. If I don't pay my property tax the government will go to a court and remove me from it just as the courts would remove me from an apartment if I did not pay the rent. Do I really own the land if someone can take it away from me simply because I don't pay them for the use of it? Could the King of England have the land taken away from him if he did not pay a tax? So long as I don't cause injury to someones person or property or defraud them shouldn't I, as a sovereign, have the right to do anything I want?

Today there are so many rules and regulations that the government has that

I think nearly everything I do is against some law. What has happened to my sovereignty? Isn't the government sovereign over me? Are there any sovereign People left in the United States of America?

There are hundreds of thousands of sovereigns in the United States of America but I am not one of them. The sovereigns own their land in "allodium." That is, the government does not have a financial interest in the their land. Because of this they do not need to pay property tax (school tax, real estate tax). Only the powers granted to the federal government in the Constitution for the United States of America define the laws that they have to follow. This is a very small subset of the laws most of us have to follow. Unless they accept benefits from or contract with the federal government, they do not have to pay Social Security tax, federal income tax, or resident individual state income tax. They do not need to register their cars or get a driver's license unless they drive commercially. They will not have to get a Health Security Card. They can own any kind of gun without a license or permit. They do not have to use the same court system that normal people do. I am sure that most people reading this are saying to themselves that this can not be true. I know I did when I first heard of it.

The government recognizes two distinct classes of citizens: a state Citizen and a federal citizen.

A state Citizen, also called a de jure Citizen, is an individual whose inalienable natural rights are recognized, secured, and protected by his/her state Constitution against State actions and against federal intrusion by the Constitution for the United States of America.

A federal citizen, also called: a 14th Amendment citizen, a citizen of the United States, a US citizen, a citizen of the District of Columbia, has civil rights that are almost equal to the natural rights that state Citizens have. I say almost because civil rights are created by Congress and can be taken away by Congress. Federal citizens are subjects of Congress, under their protection as a "resident" of a State, a person enfranchised to the federal government (the incorporated United States defined in Article I, section 8, clause 17 of the Constitution). The individual States may not deny to these persons any federal privileges or immunities that Congress has granted them. This specific class of citizen is a federal citizen under admiralty law (International Law). As such they do not have inalienable common rights recognized, secured and protected in the Constitutions of the States, or of the Constitution for the United States of America, such as "allodial" (absolute) rights to property, the rights to inheritance, the rights to work and contract, and the right to travel among others.

A federal citizen is a taxable entity like a corporation, and is subject to pay an excise tax for the privileges that Congress has granted him/her.

The rights that most people believe they have are not natural rights but civil rights which are actually privileges granted by Congress. Some of these civil rights parallel the protection of the Bill of Rights (the first 10 Amendments to the Constitution), but by researching the civil rights act along with case law decisions involving those rights, it can be shown that these so-called civil rights do not include the Ninth or Tenth Amendments and have only limited application with regard to Amendments One through Eight.

If you accept any benefit from the federal government or you claim any civil right, you are making an "adhesion contract" with the federal government. You may not be aware of any adhesion contracts but the courts are. The other aspect of such a contract is that you will obey every statute that Congress passes.

State Citizens cannot be subjected to any jurisdiction of law outside the Common Law without their knowing and willing consent after full disclosure of the terms and conditions, and such consent must be under agreement/contract sealed by signature. This is because the Constitution is a compact/contract created and existing in the jurisdiction of the Common Law, therefore, any rights secured thereunder or disabilities limiting the powers of government also exist in the Common Law, and in no other jurisdiction provided for in that compact!

Federal citizens are presumed to be operating in the jurisdiction of commercial law because that is the jurisdiction of their creator -- Congress. This is evidenced by the existence of various contracts and the use of negotiable instruments. All are products of international law or commercial law[Uniform Commercial Code]. Under Common Law your intent is important; in a court of contract (commercial law) the only thing that matters is that you live up to the letter of the contract. Because you have adhesion contracts with Congress, you can not use the Constitution or Bill of Rights as a defense because it is irrelevant to the contract. As stated previously, the contract says you will obey every statute passed by Congress. A federal citizen does not have access to Common Law.

To restate: state Citizens are bound and protected by the Constitution, like the founding fathers intended and like we are taught in school what citizenship means. Federal citizens have made further agreements with the federal government and are bound by these contracts.

The Constitution empowers the Federal Government to;

Operate on behalf of the several States in dealing with foreign relations and matters of treaties, trade agreements, etc., under the purview of International Law.

Exercise limited constitutional jurisdiction to interact with the several States in regulating trade, commerce, etc., between the States to insure equitable continuance of the compact.

Exercise exclusive jurisdiction of the District of Columbia, the Territories, and enclaves, in the same manner that a state exercises jurisdiction within its boundaries.

Rights are considered gifts from the Creator, and not to be disturbed by acts of man. Some of these rights were considered important enough to be specifically stated to be secured from Federal encroachment in the Bill of Rights, upon the theory that these rights existed long antecedent to the creation of the nation, and the theory that a government, left to its own devices without restriction, could and would use man made law to defeat the liberty that this

Republic was intended to represent.

I was born in one of the several states, the Oregon Commonwealth, so why am I not a state Citizen? The answer is that I was born a state Citizen but, I unknowingly gave it up to become a federal citizen so that I could receive benefits from the federal government. Some of the benefits that I received were: a Social Security Number, receiving mail sent to the state of OR, receiving mail with ZIP Codes, having FDIC insurance on the money left in a bank, and
using Federal Reserve Notes (dollar bills) without protest. This sounds crazy. Would you give away sovereign powers for benefits like these?

If you have a Social Security Number (SSN), you are not a state Citizen. In the near future, I will send papers into the District of Columbia stating that I am rescinding my application for a SSN. If I had known that applying for a SSN would affect my citizenship status, I would not have applied. I found out that Social Security is voluntary and that I can work without a SSN.

The Oregon Commonwealth is one of the "several states" described in the Constitution. The "several states" were severed from each other. The law treats the several states as independent countries. The Buck Act in 1940 created federal areas inside the states. If you live in a federal area, you are subject to federal territorial laws and the municipal laws of the District of Columbia. The Internal Revenue Service (IRS) is internal to the District of Columbia. The Oregon Commonwealth is not part of the District of Columbia, but the Commonwealth of Oregon is. OR is the name that the post office recognizes for mail sent into the Commonwealth of Oregon, which is a federal area. Or., Org., and Oregon are the names that the post office uses for mail sent into the Oregon Commonwealth, which is not a federal area. If I accept mail sent to OR, I am saying that I live in part of the District of Columbia. The same situation exists in the other states.

Your ZIP Code determines which ZIP Code region you live in. ZIP Code regions are federal areas. The IRS has adopted the ZIP Code regions as IRS regions. If you accept mail that has a ZIP Code on it, you are in a federal territory and thus subject to the IRS and all other municipal laws of the District of Columbia.

I find the most offensive trick to get me to lose my sovereignty was that if I do not protest using the only legal tender in America, the Federal Reserve Notes (FRN), also know as U.S. Dollars, I am receiving a benefit. This is a complicated trick that I will explain in detail later. Of course there are many other benefits that many people use that the sovereigns cannot. Among these are Social Security checks, welfare checks, food stamps, federally insured bank accounts, Medicaid, Medicare, and sending children to publicly funded schools.

I am not trying to get everybody to give up government benefits. If you wish to support and be supported by the federal government, much like people in other countries do, then by all means, go ahead and do so. But, if you wish to be a sovereign protected by the Bill of Rights and not pay many of the taxes that you are paying now but also not receive benefits, then there is an alternative. It is not an easy alternative. The law makers want control over you. They have made the legal system complex. It takes years for attorneys to learn the language and procedures of our legal system. Fortunately you do not need to know everything an attorney needs to know. You do need to have a basic understanding of how our legal system works. You may be surprised that it bears little resemblance to television courtroom dramas.

I also must warn you that reclaiming your state Citizenship status may have negative effects on your life. Besides the lack of benefits, such as unemployment checks, you are treated more harshly if you get convicted of a common law crime if you are a state Citizen. If you get convicted of rape and you are a federal citizen, you may get five years in an air conditioned prison with cable TV and three meals a day. If a state Citizen gets convicted, by a common law jury, of rape, he could be put to death.

All of the information describing how the United States really works and how it is supposed to work was so spread out that few people could see the big picture. The communication revolution has changed this. Computer bulletin boards across the country provided a means to share research. Tax protesters, ranchers, religious people, historians, gun owners, and others have all found pieces of the puzzle. Perhaps there are more pieces to find.

These researchers started on different legal threads. They followed and untangled the threads until they reached the source; The Constitution for the United States of America. The surprising thing is that the researchers did not know about each other but they each came to similar conclusions. Some of the minor details are being debated by researchers. The overall conclusions are described in this book. Some of their research is not described here. The longer this book is, the more unlikely it is that people unfamiliar with this subject will even attempt to read it.

If every Citizen in the colonies became a sovereign, how could any Citizen lose their sovereignty? The Citizens of each of the several states in the Union were sovereigns. But the people in a territory or in the District of Columbia were not because the territories and the District of Columbia were not in the Union. Congress had/has exclusive legislative control over these areas. The states were governed by a "constitutional republic" while the territories were ruled by a "legislative democracy". In a legislative democracy the citizens have no rights except what Congress gives them. In the constitutional republics, the Citizens have rights given to them by their Creator and Congress is the Citizens servant. This is why Citizens, having left a state to buy or conquer land from the native Americans, would apply for statehood as soon as possible.

How is it that someone who was born in and has lived in a state all his/her life can be treated like a citizen of the District of Columbia? There has been a series of steps that Congress has made to convert the state Citizens into federal citizens. Over the years, our laws have been made unreadable by the average intelligent person. The 14th Amendment was illegally passed, creating a federal citizen who can not question the federal debt. The Federal Reserve Act of 1913 turned over our money to a private banking cartel. Social Security created Social Security Districts (or territories) in which people with SSN lived. The Buck Act created federal areas inside the states. Let's describe each of these steps in detail.

Reasons I believe this

To show that Congress has made the laws unreadable by the average person, an objective method of measuring the readability of English text must be discussed. English scholars use a scale known as the "Flesch Index" that measures the level of understanding necessary for an individual to comprehend the written English language. Newspapers are written at an average comprehension level of 7. The average high school graduate reads and understands at a level of 10. The average law school graduate reads and comprehends at a level of 15. The Internal Revenue Code ranks on this index at an average level of 31, with some specific provisions as high as 55. And the words that are used in the law have specific legal definitions that are different from the common English definitions. If the laws that we are supposed to obey are written at a level that an individual of reasonable intelligence cannot understand then perhaps we should be highly suspect of the law writer's motives. My word processor's grammar checker tells me that this paper is written at level 11.5. People in this country cannot understand at this level. How many people have the time, energy, and ability to go into a law library and piece this together? By making the law so difficult to read, Congress has effectively removed our access to it.

To show how the government uses common English words in such a way that they have meanings that are different from what you might think, I will show how the word 'state' is redefined. In the IRS code, it says you are subject to the income tax if you live in: one of the states, the District of Columbia, Puerto Rico, Quam, or the northern Marranara Islands. From this definition it sounds as if I need to pay income tax. But, if you look at how the IRS defines the word state you probably will be confused. In the definition of the word state, it uses the word state. If you check this definition in years back you will see it has been modified several times. Before Alaska was admitted into the Union, it was in this list of states. After it became one of the states of the Union, it was not listed in the IRS definition of a state. The same thing happened to Hawaii. What does this mean? The definition that is used in the IRS code for the word state, is not a state like Texas but a state like Quam, that is a federal territory. The Federal Zone is a book listed in the other source's section of this book describes this and other words that have specific legal definitions that are, sometimes, the opposite of the common definition.

So far I have stated some unconventional ideas. To substantiate them I will cite standing decisions made by the courts and statutes passed by Congress. Unless the decision or statute is in quotation marks, it has been paraphrased. Please look up the decision or statutes to verify my paraphrase. At the end of this book, I will give the names of books and publications that give more information on the subject. One of the books will teach you how to find and understand the law. As King, we must start asking the right questions.

"People of a state are entitled to all rights which formerly belonged to the king by his prerogative." Lansing v. Smith, 21 D. 89.

"At the revolution, the sovereignty devolved on the people; and they are truly the sovereigns of the country, but they are sovereigns without subjects, and have none to govern but themselves: the citizens of America are equal as fellow citizens, and as joint tenants in the sovereignty." Chisholm Exp v. Georgia (US) 2 Dale 419, 454; I L Ed 440, 445 @DALL 1793 pp 471-472.

"as general rule men have natural right to do anything which their inclinations may suggest, if it be not evil in itself, and in no way impairs the rights of others." In Re Newman (1925), 71 C.A. 386, 235 P. 664.

"The United States government is a foreign corporation with respect to a state." In re Merriam, 36 N.E. 505, 141 N.Y. 479, affirmed 16 S.Ct. 1073, 163 U.S. 625, 41 L.Ed. 287; 20 C.J.S., Section 1785. Title 28, United States Code, Section 297 defines the several States of the union as being "freely associated compact states" in subsection (a), and then refers to these freely associated compact states as being "countries" in subsection(b). Did you know that the individual states were considered to be foreign countries to the United States and to each other?

In 1818, the Supreme Court stated that "In the United States of America, there are two (2) separated and distinct jurisdictions, such being the jurisdiction of the states within their own state boundaries, and the other being federal jurisdiction (United States), which is limited to the District of Columbia, the U.S. Territories, and federal enclaves within the states, under Article I, Section 8, Clause 17." U.S. v. Bevans, 16 U.S. (3 WHEAT) 336 (1818), reaff. 19 U.S.C.A., section 1401(h).

When Congress is operating in its exclusive jurisdiction over the District of Columbia, the Territories, and enclaves, it is important to remember that it has full authority to enact legislation as private acts pertaining to its boundaries, and it is not a state of the union of States because it exists solely by virtue of the compact/constitution that created it. The constitution does not say that the District of Columbia must guarantee a Republican form of Government to its own subject citizens within its territories. (See Hepburn & Dundas v. Ellzey, 6 US. 445(1805); Glaeser v. Acacia Mut. Life Ass'n., 55 F. Supp., 925 (1944); Long v. District of Columbia, 820 F.2d 409 (D.C. Cir. 1987); Americana of Puerto Rico, Inc. v. Kaplus, 368 F.2d 431 (1966), among others).

"The idea prevails with some -- indeed, it found expression in arguments at the bar -- that we have in this country substantially or practically two national governments; one, to be maintained under the Constitution, with all its restrictions; the other to be maintained by

Congress outside and independently of that instrument, by exercising such powers as other nations of the earth are accustomed to exercise." Downes v. Bidwell, 182 U.S. 244, supra. The Constitution provides limited powers to federal government over the state Citizens. The federal government has unlimited powers over federal citizens because it is acting outside of the Constitution. Administrative laws are private acts and are not applicable to state Citizens. The Internal Revenue Code is administrative law.

"We are a republic. Real liberty is never found in despotism or in the extremes of democracy." - Alexander Hamilton.

The origin of the federal citizen

So far I have not given any proof that the government actually recognizes two distinct classes of citizens. I will give that evidence now by describing the 13th and 14th Amendments.

In 1865, the 13th Amendment abolished slavery and involuntary servitude except as punishment for a crime. The Supreme Court ruled that the 13th Amendment operated to free former slaves and prohibit slavery, but it in no way conferred citizenship to the former slaves, or to those of races other than white, because the founders of the Constitution were all of the white race.

The federal government did not have the authority to determine if former slaves could become a Citizen of one of the several states because the 9th and 10th Amendments said that powers not granted specifically to the federal government by the Constitution are reserved to the states or to the People. History shows that the Pennsylvania Commonwealth and New York State were nationalizing blacks as State Citizens. In other states blacks were not Citizens and therefore did not have standing in any court. The answer to this problem was the 14th Amendment.

The 14th Amendment used the term "citizen of the United States." The courts have ruled that this means federal citizenship which is similar to a citizen of the District of Columbia. Since the federal government didn't step in and tell Pennsylvania or New York that it couldn't make State Citizens out of former black slaves, an argument could be made that the 14th Amendment was written primarily to afford [voluntary] citizenship to those of the black race that were recently freed by the 13th Amendment (Slaughter-House Cases, 16 Wall. 36, 71), and did not include Indians and others NOT born in and subject to the jurisdiction of the United States (McKay v. Cambell, 2 Sawy. 129), Thus, the Amendment recognized that "an individual can be a Citizen of one of the several States without being a citizen of the United States," (U.S. v. Anthony, 24 Fed. Cas. 829, 830), or, "a citizen of the United States without being a Citizen of a State." (Slaughter-House Cases, supra; cf. U.S. v. Cruikshank, 92 US 542, 549 (1875)).

To restate: In the Slaughter-House Cases, supra the Court said: "It is quite clear, then, that there is a citizenship of the United States and a citizenship of a state, which are distinct from each other and which depend upon different characteristics or circumstances of the individual. . . . Of the privileges and immunities of the citizens of the United States and of the privileges and immunities of the citizen of the state, and what they respectfully are, we will presently consider; but we wish to state here that it is only the former which are placed by this clause under the protection of the Federal Constitution, and the latter, whatever they may be, are not intended to have any additional protection by this paragraph of the amendment."

The court has also ruled that "The term United States is a metaphor [a figure of speech]". Cunard S.S Co. V. Mellon, 262 US 100, 122; and that "The term 'United States' may be used in one of several senses. It may be merely the name of a sovereign occupying the position analogous to that of sovereign in a family of nations. It may designate territory over which sovereignty of the United States extends, or it may be a collective name of the states which are united by and under the Constitution." Hooven & Allison Co. v. Evatt, 324 US 652, 672-73.

Did the Courts really say that someone could be a Citizen of a State without being a citizen of the United States? Yes, they did. It's true that the cases cited above are old, some over 100 years old. None of these cases have ever been overturned by a more recent decision, so they are valid. A more recent case is Crosse v. Bd. of Supervisors, 221 A.2d 431 (1966) which says: "Both before and after the Fourteenth Amendment to the federal Constitution, it has not been necessary for a person to be a citizen of the United States in order to be a citizen of his state." Citing U.S. v. Cruikshank, supra.

The courts presume you to be a federal citizen, without even telling you that there are different classes of citizens. It is up to you dispute this. "Unless the defendant can prove he is not a citizen of the United States, the IRS has the right to inquire and determine a tax liability." U.S. v. Slater, 545 Fed. Supp. 179,182 (1982).

In 1866, Congress passed the first civil rights act which only applied to the District of Columbia and other federal territories. In 1868, the 14th Amendment was proclaimed to be passed. At this point the number of subjects that the federal government had exclusive jurisdiction over increased to all of the former slaves that had not become state Citizens. There are many reasons why I do not like the 14th Amendment. The first is that is was never ratified!

"I cannot believe that any court in full possession of all its faculties, would ever rule that the (14th) Amendment was properly approved and adopted." State v. Phillips, 540 P.2d. 936; Dyett v. Turner, 439 P.2d. 266. (The court in this case was the Utah Supreme Court.) Further, in 1967, Congress tried to repeal the 14th Amendment on the ground that it is invalid, void, and unconstitutional. CONGRESSIONAL RECORD -- HOUSE, June 13, 1967, pg. 15641. The nine pages of argument that are recorded here detail the infirmities that prove that the 14th Amendment was never properly ratified, and thus is no law!

The 14th Amendment reads in pertinent part, "All persons, born or naturalized in the United States, and subject to the jurisdiction thereof, are citizens of the United States and of the State wherein they reside....The validity of the public debt of the United States...shall not be questioned."

There is a wealth of deception in the above wording, because of sheer number of words that have specific or multiple meanings in law depending upon how they are used.

Go the part "and subject to the jurisdiction thereof." The word the is used in a singular form, not the plural, as is the word jurisdiction. If Congress meant the several States, rather that the District of Columbia, it would have been more correct to say "and subject to their jurisdictions."

In addition, a new pecking order is established with the phrase. "are citizens of the United States and of the State wherein they reside."

If you research the terms "resident" and "legal residence", you find that it is the nexus that binds us all to the State and federal enforcement of commercial law statutes today. "Resident" is the short form of "Resident Alien" and is used in State statutes to mean someone who exhibits actual presence in an area belonging to one nation while retaining a domicile/citizenship status within another foreign nation [The United States/District of Columbia]. The term "legal residence" further indicates that these two terms may be applied either to a geographical jurisdiction, or, a political jurisdiction. An individual may reside in one or the other, or in both at the same time. In California, Government Code, section 126, sets forth the essential elements of a compact between this State and the federal government allowing reciprocal taxation of certain entities, and provide for concurrent jurisdiction within geographical boundaries.

Both state Citizens and federal citizens are Americans. US citizens are "domiciled" in the District of Columbia and are privileged alien to the state wherein the reside and state Citizens are domiciled in their state and not aliens in their state. They also do not reside in their state;

they are Citizens of the state. The distinction may seem insignificant to you but it is not to the court. A state Citizen has the right to travel in each of the 50 states. He/she can file papers at any county courthouse in any state and become a Citizen of that state.

Most of the federal statute laws do not apply to Citizens of a state. If the authority for the statute can be found in the organic Constitution, then the statute is of a National character, as it applies to both state Citizens and aliens.

"Upon introducing the provisions which eventually became 18 U.S.C. 242, its sponsor, Senator Stewart, explicitly stated that the bill protected all 'persons'... He noted that the bill 'simply extends to foreigners, not citizens, the protection of our laws'." United States v. Otherson, 480 F.Supp. 1369, 1373 (1979). What could this mean? Well, it implies that Citizens of a state already had the protections introduced by this statute, but it extended to foreigners this protection also. What is a "foreigner" if they are not also an "alien"?

Privileges granted by the sovereign (governments) in their capacity to license (condone) what might otherwise be illegal are always taxable and regulatable. Rights such as those envisioned by the founding fathers are not taxable or regulatable because they are exercises of the common right that could be completely destroyed by government through taxation and/or regulation. These are maxims of law so well established that they are irrefutable. For example, look to Frost & Frost Trucking v. Railroad Commission of California, 271 U.S. 583, 70 L.Ed. 1101 (1925).

Now, in 1868, we have a class of citizenship created [14th Amendment] which is "subject" by grant of privilege from a sovereign power [federal Congress] exercising exclusive authority to govern its territory under Article I, sect. 8, cl. 17 of the Constitution. Federal citizens are created by Congress. It is self-evident that all state Citizens are created equal; that they are endowed, by their creator, with certain inalienable rights, and that governments are instituted to secure these rights.

It is also a self-evident truth that the sovereign creator can never create an entity (government) and assign it more power than what the creator possesses to begin with. Further, the Constitution for the United States of America did not repeal the Articles of Confederation, it was only intended "to make a more perfect union." Therefore, it logically follows that the creator did not purposely intend to alter their status as MASTER to accept a role as SERVANT to its own creation. This is plainly shown throughout the Constitution, but especially set forth in the Tenth Amendment. (cf. United States v. Darby, 312 U.S. 100, 124 (1941); Cooper v. Aaron, 358 U.S. 1 (1958))

"The right to tax and regulate the national citizenship is an inherent right under the rule of the Law of Nations, which is part of the law of the United States, as described in Article 1, Section 8, Clause 17." The Luisitania, 251 F.715, 732. And, "This jurisdiction extends to citizens of the United States, wherever resident, for the exercise of the privileges and immunities and protections of [federal] citizenship." Cook v. Tait, (1924) 265 U.S. 37,44 S.Ct 447, 11 Virginia Law Review, 607."

The right of trial by jury in civil cases, guaranteed by the 7th Amendment (walker v. Sauvinet, 92 U.S. 90), and the right to bear arms, guaranteed by the 2nd Amendment (presser v. Illinois, 116 U.S. 252), have been distinctly held not to be privileges and immunities of citizens of the United States guaranteed by the 14th Amendment against abridgment by the states, and in effect the same decision was made in respect of the guarantee against prosecution, except by indictment of a grand jury, contained in the 5th Amendment (Hurtado v. California, 110 U.S. 516), and in respect of the right to be confronted with witnesses, contained in the 6th Amendment." West v. Louisianna, 194 U.S. 258.

The privileges and immunities [civil rights] of the 14th Amendment citizens were derived [taken] from....the Constitution, but are not identical to those referred to in Article IV, sect. 2 of the Constitution [which recognizes the existence of state Citizens who were not citizens of the

United States because there was no such animal in 1787]. Plainly spoken, RIGHTS considered to be grants from our creator are clearly different from the "civil rights" that were granted by Congress to its own brand of franchised citizen in the 14th Amendment.

"A 'civil right' is a right given and protected by law [man's law], and a person's enjoyment thereof is regulated entirely by law that creates it." Nickell v. Rosenfield, (1927) 82 CA 369, 375, 255 P. 760.

Title 42 of the USC contains the Civil Rights laws. It says "Rights under 42 USCS section 1983 are for citizens of the United States and not of state. Wadleigh v. Newhall (1905, CC Cal) 136 F 941."

In summary, what we are talking about here is a Master-Servant relationship. Prior to the 14th Amendment, there were state Citizens and non-citizens. State Citizens were the masters in the relationship to government. After the 14th Amendment was declared to be passed, a new class of citizenship was created, which is both privileged and servant [subject] to the creator [the federal government].

How state Citizens were converted into federal citizens

In order for the federal government to tax a Citizen of one of the several states, it had to create some sort of contractual nexus. This contractual nexus is the Social Security Number (SSN).

In 1935, the federal government instituted Social Security. The Social Security Board then created 10 Social Security "Districts." The combination of these "Districts" resulted in a "Federal Area", a fictional jurisdiction, which covered all of the several states like a clear plastic overlay.

In 1939, the federal government instituted the "Public Salary Tax Act of 1939." This Act is a municipal law of the District of Columbia for taxing all federal government employees and those who live and work in any "Federal Area." Now the government knows it cannot tax those state Citizens who live and work outside the territorial jurisdiction of Article 1, Section 8, Clause 2 in the Constitution for the United States of America; also known as the ten square miles of the District of Columbia and territories and enclaves. So, in 1940, Congress passed the "Buck Act" now found in 4 U.S.C. Sections 105-113. In Section 110(e), this Act authorized any department of the federal government to create a "Federal Area" for imposition of the "Public Salary Tax Act of 1939." This tax is imposed at 4 U.S.C. Section 111. The rest of the taxing law is found in the Internal Revenue Code. The Social Security Board had already created a "Federal Area" overlay. U.S.C. Title 4 is as follows:

Sec. 110(d): The term "State" includes any territory or possession of the United States.

Sec. 110(e): The term "Federal Area" means any lands or premises held or acquired by or for the use of the United states or any department, establishment, or agency of the United states; and any federal area, or any part thereof, which is located within the exterior boundaries of any State, shall be deemed to be a federal area located within such State.

Under the Provisions of Title 4, Section 105, the federal "State" (also known as, "The State of...") is imposing an excise tax. That section states, in pertinent part:

Sec. 105: State, and so forth, taxation affecting Federal areas; sales or use tax.

(a) No person shall be relieved from the liability for payment of, collection of, or accounting for any sales or use tax levied by any State, or any duly constituted taxing authority therein, having jurisdiction to levy such tax, on the ground that the sales or use, with respect to which such tax is levied, occurred in whole or in part within a Federal area; and such State or taxing authority shall have full jurisdiction to levy such a tax, by reason of his residing within a Federal area or receiving income from transactions occurring or services performed in such area; and such State or taxing authority shall have full jurisdiction and power to levy and collect such tax in any Federal area within such a State to the same extent and with the same effect as though such area was not a Federal area.

NOTE: Irrespective of what the tax is called, if its purpose is to produce revenue, it is an income tax or a receipts tax under the Buck Act [4 U.S.C. Secs. 105-110]. See Humble Oil & Refining Co. v. Calvert, 464 SW 2d. 170 (1971), affd (Tex) 478 SW 2d. 926, cert. den. 409 U.S. 967, 34 L.Ed. 2d 234, 93 S.Ct. 293.

For purposes of further explanation, a Federal area can include the Social Security areas designated by the Social Security Administration; any public housing that has federal funding; a home that has a federal (or Federal reserve) loan; a road that has federal funding; schools and colleges (public or private) that receive (direct or indirectly) federal funding, and virtually everything that the federal government touches through any type of direct or indirect aid. See Springfield v. Kenny, 104 N.E. 2d. 65 (1951 app.) This "Federal area" is attached to anyone who has a Social Security number or any personal contact with the federal or State government. (That is, of course, with the exception of those who have been defrauded through the tenets of an Unrevealed Contract to "accept" compelled benefits. Which includes me and perhaps you.) Through this mechanism, the federal government usurped the Sovereignty of the People, as well as the Sovereignty of the several states by creating "Federal areas" within the authority of Article IV, Section 3, Clause 2 in the Constitution for the United States of America which states:

"The Congress shall have Power to dispose of and make all needful Rules and Regulations respecting the Territory or other Property belonging to the United States, and nothing in this Constitution shall be so construed as to prejudice any claims of the United states, or of any particular State."

Therefore, all U.S. citizens [i.e. citizens of the District of Columbia] residing in one of the states of the Union, are classified as property and franchisees of the federal government, and as an "individual entity." See Wheeling Steel Corp. v. Fox 298 U.S. 193, 80 L.Ed. 1143, 56 S.Ct. 773. Under the "Buck Act," 4 U.S.C Secs. 105-113, the federal government has created a "Federal area" within the boundaries of the several states. This area is similar to any territory that the federal government acquires through purchase, conquest or treaty, thereby imposing federal territorial law upon the people in this "Federal area." Federal territorial law is evidenced by the Executive Branch's Admiralty flag (a federal flag with a gold or yellow fringe on it) flying in schools, offices and courtrooms.

To enjoy the freedoms secured by the federal and state constitutions, you must live on the land in one of the states of the Union of several states, not in any "Federal area." Nor can you be involved in any activity that makes you subject to "federal laws." You cannot have a valid Social Security Number, a "resident" State driver's license, a motor vehicle registered in your name, a bank account in a federally insured bank, or any other known "contract implied in fact" that would place you in this "Federal area" and thus within the territorial jurisdiction of the municipal laws of Congress. Remember, all acts of Congress are territorial in nature and can only apply within the territorial jurisdiction of Congress. See American Banana Co. v. United fruit Co., 213 U.S. 347, 356-357 (1909); U.S. v. Spelar, 338 U.S. 217, 222, 94 L.Ed. 3, 70 S.Ct. 402 (1925).

This is not easy to do! Most banks are federally insured. It may be inconvenient to bank at an institution that is not federally insured. There are many things that become a little more difficult to do without a SSN, driver's licenses, or a ZIP Code.

There has been created a fictional federal "State (of) within a state." See Howard v. Sinking Fund of Louisville, 344 U.S. 624, 73 S.Ct. 465, 476, 97 L.Ed. 617 (1953); Schwarts v. O'Hara TP School District, 100 A 2d. 621, 625, 375, Pa. 440. Compare also 31 C.F.R. Parts 51.2 and 52.2, which also identify a fictional State within a state. This fictional "State" is identified by the use of two-letter abbreviations like "PA", "NJ", "AZ", and "DE", etc., as distinguished from the authorized abbreviations for the sovereign States: "Pa.", "N.J.", "Ariz.", and "Del." The fictional States also use ZIP Codes that are within the municipal, exclusive legislative jurisdiction of

Congress. The Pennsylvania Commonwealth is one of the several States. The Commonwealth of Pennsylvania, also known as PA, is a subdivision of the District of Columbia. If you accept postal matter sent to PA, and/or with a ZIP Code, the Courts say that this is evidence that you are a federal citizen or a resident. Use of the Zip Code is voluntary. See Domestic Mail Service Regulations, Section 122.32. The Postal service cannot discriminate against the non-use of the ZIP Code. See Postal Reorganization Act, Section 403, (Public Law 91-375). The IRS has adopted the ZIP Code areas as Internal Revenue Districts. See the Federal Register, Volume 51, Number 53, Wednesday March 19, 1986. The acceptance of mail with a ZIP Code is one of the requirements for the IRS to have jurisdiction to send you notices.

When you apply for a Social Security Number, you are telling the federal government that you are repudiating your state Citizenship in order to apply for the benefits of citizenship in the federal Nation. Granting a Social Security number is prima facie evidence that no matter what you were before, you have voluntarily entered into a voyage for profit or gain in negotiable instruments and maritime enterprise. This is the system that has been set up over the years to restrict, control, and destroy our personal and economic liberties. Our legal system is very complicated and you may not understand how it works. I believe that this is intentional.

Common law versus commercial law

Besides the municipal laws for federal territory like the District of Columbia, the Constitution specifies three other types of law: Common Law, Equity Law, and Admiralty Law.
Common Law is criminal law. Equity Law deals with written contracts and is civil law.
Admiralty Law deals with international contracts and has both criminal and civil penalties.
A cursory review of the Uniform Commercial Code proves that it was codified to replace the Negotiable Instrument Laws. Further research reveals that the Negotiable Instrument Laws have their foundation in the jurisdiction of Admiralty Law (Maritime Law -- law of the sea), and,

the U.C.C. has come to be known in law as the substantive common law. (Bank v. Moore, 201 Ala. 411, 78 So. 789) This substantive common law has also been directly tied to the jurisdiction of the Law Merchant [International Law]. (Miller v. Miller, 296 SW.2d 648).

Under the Common Law, every contract must be entered into knowingly, voluntarily, and intentionally by both parties or it is void and unenforceable. Common Law contracts must also be based on substance. For example, contracts used to read, "For one dollar and other valuable considerations, I will paint your house, etc." That was a valid contract...the dollar was a genuine silver dollar. Now suppose you wrote a contract that said "For one Federal Reserve Note and other considerations..." And suppose, for example, I painted your house the wrong color. Could you go into a Common Law court and get justice? No, you could not. You see, a Federal Reserve Note is a "colorable" dollar, as it has no substance, and in a Common Law jurisdiction, that contract would be unenforceable.

The word colorable means something that appears to be genuine but is not. If it looks like a dollar, and spends like a dollar but is not redeemable for lawful money (silver or gold) it is colorable. If a federal Reserve Note is used in a contract, then the contract becomes a colorable contract. And colorable contracts must be enforced under a colorable jurisdiction. So by creating Federal Reserve Notes, the government had to create a jurisdiction to cover the kinds of contracts that use them. We now have what is called Statutory Jurisdiction which is not a genuine Admiralty Jurisdiction. It is colorable Admiralty Jurisdiction the judges are enforcing because we are using colorable money.

This government set up a "colorable" law system to fit the colorable currency. It used to be called the Law Merchant or the Law of Redeemable instruments because it dealt with paper that was redeemable in something of substance. But, once Federal Reserve Notes had become unredeemable, there had to be a system of law which was completely colorable from start to finish. This system of law was codified as the Uniform Commercial Code, and has been adopted in every state.

One difference between Common Law and the Uniform Commercial Code (UCC) is that in Common Law, contracts must be entered into: knowingly, voluntarily, and intentionally. Under the UCC, this is not so. First of all, contracts are unnecessary. Under this new law, "agreements" can be binding, and if you only exercise the benefits of an "agreement," it is presumed or implied that you intend to meet the obligations associated with those benefits. If you accept a benefit offered by government, then you are obligated to follow, to the letter, each and every statute involved with that benefit. The trick has been to get everybody exercising benefits that they don't believe they can live without.

One "benefit" that I accepted was the privilege of discharging debt with limited liability, instead of paying debt. When I pay a debt, I give substance for substance. If I buy a quart of milk with a silver dollar, that dollar bought the milk, and the milk bought the dollar -- substance for substance. But if I used a Federal Reserve Note to buy the milk, I have not paid for it. There is no substance in the Federal Reserve Note. It is worthless paper given in exchange for something of substantive value. Congress offers this benefit. Debt money, created by the federal United States, can be spent all over the continental united States; it will be legal tender for all debts, public and private, and the limited liability is that I cannot be sued for not paying my debts. It's as if they have said, "We're going to help you out, and you can discharge your debts instead of paying your debts." When I use this colorable money to discharge my debts, I cannot use a Common Law court. I can only use a colorable court. It would appear that I am stuck. If the only legal tender is colorable money, then if I use any legal tender, then the only court that is available to me is a colorable court. But there is a way out.

Volume 1, Section 207 of the Uniform Commercial Code states "The making of a valid Reservation of Rights preserves whatever rights the person then possesses, and prevents the loss of such rights by application of concepts of waiver or estoppel." (UCC 1-207.7) It also says "When a waivable right or claim is involved, the failure to make a reservation thereof, causes a loss of the right, and bars its assertion at a later date." (UCC 1-207.4) It also says "The Sufficiency of the Reservation--Any expression indicating an intention to reserve such rights, is sufficient, such as "without prejudice." (UCC 1-207.4)

Whenever I sign any legal paper that deals with Federal Reserve Notes--in any way, shape or manner--under my signature I write, or stamp: "Without Prejudice UCC 1-207." When I use "without prejudice UCC 1-207" in connection with my signature, I am saying: "I reserve my right not to be compelled to perform under any contract or commercial agreement that I did not enter knowingly, voluntarily, and intentionally. And furthermore, I do not accept the liability of the compelled benefit of any unrevealed contract or commercial agreement." Some people use a rubber stamp that says "DISCHARGED WITHOUT PREJUDICE UCC 1-207" on every Federal Reserve Note that pass through their hands. I do not think this is necessary.

What is the compelled performance of an unrevealed commercial agreement? When I use Federal Reserve Notes instead of silver dollars, is it voluntary? No. There is no lawful money, so I have to use Federal Reserve Notes--I have to accept the benefit. The government has given me the benefit to discharge my debts with limited liability. Therefore discharging my debts instead of paying my debts is a compelled benefit.

The Uniform Commercial Code says in Volume 1, Section 103.6: "The Code is complimentary to the Common Law, which remains in force, except where displaced by the code. A statute should be construed in harmony with the Common Law, unless there is a clear legislative intent to abrogate the Common Law." It also says: "The Code cannot be read to preclude a Common Law action."

Most court proceedings today are under a colorable Admiralty jurisdiction also known as Statutory jurisdiction. In Admiralty jurisdiction, "The technical niceties of the common law are not regarded...", 1 R.C.L. 31, p. 422. "A jury does not figure, ordinarily, in the trial of an admiralty suit...the verdict of the jury merely advisory, and may be disregarded by the court." 1 R.C.L. 40, p. 432. "[The] rules of practice may be altered whenever found to be inconvenient or likely to embarrass the business of the court." 1 R.C.L. 32, p. 423. "A court of admiralty ... acts upon equitable principles." 1 R.C.L. 17, p. 416. Have you ever heard a court case where the judge overrules the decision of the jury? This can only happen in a trial in admiralty jurisdiction. The jury is only the conscience of the court. The judge is not an impartial referee who understands Public Law but a commissioner that supports Public Policy which is private law. And your attorney may not be working for you. In CORPUS JURIS SECUNDUM (complete restatement of the entire American law) Volume 7, section 4 states: "an attorney occupies a dual position which imposes dual obligations. His first duty is to the courts and the public not to the client and wherever the duties to his client conflict with those he owes as an officer of the court in the administration of justice, the former must yield to the latter....Clients are also called 'wards of the court'." The fifth edition of Blacks Law Dictionary states that a Ward of court is: "person of unsound mind".

What does this mean? If you don't know how the legal system works you will be treated like a person of unsound mind that hires an expensive attorney, who is an officer of the court, to defend you, and that if the judge does not want to hear your arguments, he can command the attorney, without your knowledge, not to use the defense, and the judge does not let the jury read the law, he only gives his interpretation of the law, and that the laws are usually part of very large bills that are not even read by members of Congress who voted on it, and that if, in the unlikely event that the jury comes to conclusions that the judge does not agree with, the judge can overturn the decision of the jury. As bad as this is, it is not the worst case scenario.

If you are accused of breaking certain administrative laws, such as driving infractions, you do not have the right to even this type of jury trial. In Tax Court, you are actually suing the IRS which is presumed innocent until you prove that they are guilty. Because of this you do not have the right to have council of your choice. Only the defendant has the right to council. The judges are the most successful former prosecutors in Tax Court. Is this the way our legal system was supposed to work? No! In Common Law the jury determines both the facts and the law, the judge is an impartial referee, and the council for both the Plaintiff and defendant are working for their clients. If you know how the legal system works and you are a state Citizen, you will challenge the jurisdiction of the court and never go into anything but a Common Law court. If the flag in the courtroom has a gold fringe on it, you are in an admiralty court.

The jury can nullify a law. The two most notable times in the history of the United States were the end of slavery and the end of prohibition. Hiding escaped slaves was against the federal law (stolen property transferred across state lines). People arrested for hiding runaway slaves would be tried. In many cases the jury would find the defendant not guilty because the law was not valid. The same thing happened to bootleggers during prohibition. If a prosecutor can not get a jury to convict people of crimes then the law has been effectively nullified. This was a way Citizens defended their sovereignty from the government. If the government passed a law that the Citizens disagreed with, they would nullify it when someone was tried for breaking the law. This is the way the country was supposed to be. By trying cases in admiralty jurisdiction the jury can still try to nullify a law but the judge can overrule the decision made by the jury. In many cases, the judge incorrectly tells the jury they must follow the instructions to the jury. If Citizens can not nullify laws, the federal government has more power.

From the last few paragraphs, you may think that I do not have a high opinion of the integrity of our judges. This is not correct. The courts are there to resolve disputes without violence.

Since the vast majority of the people in this country are either US citizens or residents, judges are correct to assume that everyone that comes before them are under the exclusive jurisdiction of Congress. It is up to the Citizen to challenge the jurisdiction of an admiralty court.

So if you are a state Citizen and you take precautions of not making it easy for the federal government to make the presumption that you are involved in an international contract, such as Federal Reserve Notes, then you will not be able to be charged with any statutory offenses. You will be able to do anything you wish, so long as you do not use force or fraud and you live with the consequences of your actions.

More federal glue

You may also find it disturbing to know how an administrative procedure can remove your children from you. In 1921 Congress passed the Sheppard-Towner Maternity Act that created the United States birth "registration" area (see Public Law 97, 67th Congress, Session I, Chapter 135, 1921.) That act allows you to register your children when they are born. If you do so, you will get a copy of the birth certificate. By registering your children, which is voluntary, they become Federal Children. This does several things: Your children become subjects of Congress (they lose their state citizenship). A copy of the birth certificate is sent to the Department of Vital Statistics in the state in which they were born. The original birth certificate is sent to the Department of Commerce in the District of Columbia. It then gets forwarded to an International Monetary Fund (IMF) building in Europe. Your child's future labor and properties are put up as collateral for the public debt.

Once a child is registered, a constructive trust is formed. The parent(s) usually become the trustee (the person managing the assets of the trust), the child becomes an asset of the trust, and the state becomes the principal beneficiary of the trust. See The Uniform Trustees' Powers Act (ORS 128.005(1)). If the beneficiary does not believe the trustee is managing the assets of the trust optimally, the beneficiary can go through an administrative procedure to change trustees. This is the way that bureaucrats can take children away from their parents if the bureaucrat does not like the way the child is cared for. You may say that there is nothing wrong with this. If a parent is neglecting a child, then the state should remove the child from the parents custody. Under common law a child can still be removed from the parent but it takes twelve jurors from that county to do so. Theoretically, a bureaucrat could remove your children from you, if you disagree with some unrelated administrative procedure, such as home schooling the child. This is another way the government can intimidate citizens who question its authority. With all this in mind, the statement that the President says every few months: "Our children are our most valuable asset." takes on a different meaning. That is - your children are their assets.

Part of the process of restoring my state Citizenship status is revoking my Birth Certificate through a process called REVOCATION OF SIGNATURE AND POWER OF ATTORNEY. If my Birth Certificate is not revoked, then the courts consider me to be a 14th Amendment federal citizen and my labor and all of my assets are put up as collateral for the public debt. When the government communicates with corporations it spells the name of the corporation in all capital letters. If the government refers to you with your name in all capital letters, it is actually means to treat you like a corporation. A corporation is created by government. It has no rights. The government gives it privileges and the corporation must follow the rules of its creator. I am not a corporation! A state Citizen should challenge the government's assertion that he/she is a corporation. This applies to both postal matter and court documents.

We gave the federal government the right to regulate commerce. Since the government has started usurping our sovereignty, our language has been subtly modified to include commercial terms. Most people do not realize or care that they are using commercial terms but the courts do. If you describe your actions in commercial terms in a court, the judge will take silent notice of your status as being regulatable by the federal government. In the following examples, the commercial terms are all in upper case letters: instead of a birthing room, you are now born in a DELIVERY room. Instead of traveling in your car, you are DRIVING or OPERATING a MOTOR VEHICLE in TRAFFIC and you don't have guests in your car, you have PASSENGERS. Instead of a nativity you have a DATE OF BIRTH. You are not a worker but an EMPLOYEE. You don't own a house but a piece of REAL ESTATE.

Lost rights

A state Citizen has the right to have any gun he/she wishes without being registered. A federal citizen does not. In the District of Columbia, it is a felony to own a handgun unless you are a police officer or a security guard or the hand gun was registered before 1978. The District of Columbia has not been admitted into the Union. Therefore the people of the District of Columbia are not protected by the Second Amendment or any other part of the Bill of Rights. Despite the lack of legal guns in DC, crime is rampant. It is called Murder Capital of the World. This should prove that gun control/victim disarmament laws do not work in America. Across the country, there is an assault on guns. If you are a federal citizen and you are using Second Amendment arguments to protect your rights to keep your guns, I believe you are in for a surprise. First by registering gun owners then renaming guns 'Assault Weapons' and 'Handguns', those in power will take away your civil right to bear arms. Of course, they won't tell you that the right to keep and bear arms is a civil right and not a natural right for a US citizens. The Supreme court has ruled that you as an individual have no right to protection by the police. Their only obligation is to protect "society". The real protection for state Citizens to keep their guns is not the Second Amendment but the Ninth Amendment. Note in Switzerland, every household must have, by law, a fully automatic machine gun and ammunition. The crime rate is very low there.

A state Citizen has the right to travel on the public easements (public roads) without being registered. A federal citizen does not. It is a privilege for a foreigner to travel in any of the several states. If you are a US citizen, you are a foreigner in the state. The state legislators can require foreigners and people involved in commerce (chauffeurs, freight haulers) to be licensed, insured, and to have their vehicles registered. When you register your car, you turn over power of attorney to the state. At that point, it becomes a motor vehicle. If it is not registered then it is not a motor vehicle and there are no motor vehicle statutes to break. There are common law rules of the road. If you don't cause an injury to anybody then you can not be tried.

If your car is registered, the state effectively owns your car. The state supplies a sticker to put on your license plate every time you re-register the motor vehicle. Look closely at the sticker on your plate right now. You may be surprised to see that it says "OFFICIAL USE ONLY". (Note: In some states, they do not use stickers on the plate) You may have seen municipal vehicles that have signs on them saying "OFFICIAL USE ONLY" on them but why does yours? You do not own your car. You may have a Certificate of Title but you probably do not have the certificate of origin. You are leasing the state's vehicle by paying the yearly registration fee. Because you are using their equipment, they can make rules up on how it can be used. If you break a rule, such as driving without a seatbelt, you have broken the contract and an administrative procedure will make you pay the penalty. A state Citizen must be able to explain to the police officers why they are not required to have the usual paperwork that most people have. They should carry copies of affidavits and other paperwork in their car. The state Citizen should also be prepared to go to traffic court and explain it to the judge.

Unanswered questions

A reasonable person may ask - How did the government get so far removed from the model of government defined by the Constitution? I'm not sure. Perhaps it was a small group of bankers who realized that they could control a central government much easier than many independent sovereigns. Perhaps it is the natural outcome of specialization; that is, it might be said that a brain surgeon should not be expected to be an expert on farming, manufacturing, mining, retailing, politics, as well as medicine, therefore it is possible that the people wanted to be governed by experts - allowing them to focus on their pleasures and careers. Perhaps the elite thought they would help the poor masses by making decisions for them because they believed that the common people could not make good decisions for themselves. Perhaps it is the result of people believing that they can get something for nothing; that is, the people believed that the government was stealing more from other citizens that it was stealing from them, so overall, they were helped by such policies more than they were hurt. There is some evidence to support each of these propositions but, one thing is important: The government is acting this way because the people allow it to. If the people were very dissatisfied with the government, they would change it. For all the complaining Americans do, they still elect the same people again and again.

Another good question is: If all this is true, why haven't I heard these ideas before? Again, I am not sure. It is very difficult to keep a conspiracy secret for very long. If there has been a plan to steal the sovereignty of the people, then many people would be affected and more than a few people had to know about the plan in order to execute it. Unless all of the politicians, bankers, media people were in on the conspiracy or were intimidated so that they would not expose the plan, the People would, sooner or later, find out. It is difficult for me to believe that every politician, banker, and media person are corrupt. I think it is more likely that people thought that the experts could run the country better than they could. Today, many people can not conceive the government being run any other way. It is my belief that turning over the government to experts was a mistake.

Who are these people?

The people who do research on state citizenship call themselves patriots. This may sound strange to people who equate patriotism with support for whatever the government does as long as the flags are waving and the politicians say have the best interest of the nation at heart, but patriots like Thomas Jefferson saw patriotism as supporting the value of liberty. The founders of the nation thought it was unpatriotic to accept being ruled by a sovereign. In the Constitutional Republic that they founded, each Citizen was a sovereign without subjects. That is, we were all equal. This did not mean that we each had an equal amount of money or an equal standard of living. Each Citizen had equal opportunity to use the gifts we were given at birth. If you did not use your gifts wisely or you did not have many gifts to start with, then you had to accept a lower standard of living. People who received charity were not treated with the same respect as a person who did not.

How does one reclaim their state Citizenship?

This book cannot give you everything you need to know on how to restore your first class citizenship status. It is only a starting point. With that being said, here is a list of the papers that a state Citizen should file accordingly, to be free of federal adhesion contracts. Some of these things are to be done at the county recorder's office, others must be sent to the District of Columbia.

A notice of intent

A declaration of sovereignty.

An oath to your state.

A notice that you are using Federal Reserve Notes under protest.

A revocation of

1. signature and power of attorney

2. driver's license (you don't need one unless you drive commercially)

3. motor vehicle registration (if your car is not registered, it is not a motor vehicle)

4. marriage license (but not your marriage contract)

5. birth certificate (the hospital still has a record of birth)

6. application for a Social Security Number

7. union membership

8. status as an employee (the word employee has a specific legal definition)

9. voter registration (you become an elector not a voter)

10. private or public pension benefits

You should also close credit cards, saving accounts, checking accounts, IRA accounts, money market accounts, CD's, mutual funds, and 401k. You should pay off all mortgages, car loans, and any other loan that you have. You may continue to receive postal matter with ZIP codes but you should not accept them. You should also remove your children from the schools that receive public money.

This is not easy! But, you can do it. If only a few people were doing this it would be very difficult. But hundreds of thousands have done this just in the past few years. This makes it much easier since alternative organizations are being formed that are servicing the non federal citizens. Note: there are some banks that have been around for more than 100 years that are safe and not federally insured. Also common law trusts can be created to circumvent some of the restrictions that the list above implies. There are many intelligent and creative people working on these problems. As the years go by, it will be more and more difficult to remain federal citizens. As the number of state Citizens increases, the amount of revenue that the federal government receives will decrease. The amount of money that the federal government spends will probably not decrease because most of the people reclaiming their state Citizenship don't use the services provided by the federal government. This will cause taxes to increase which will cause even more people to drop out of the federal system. I also expect to see the continuation of the trend to add more regulations that the federal citizens have to follow.

Other sources of information

The best source of information is a law library. you can find a law library that is open to the public in you county courthouse. You may find better law libraries at a local college. The problem with the law library is that there are so many books in it. Some of the court cases cited here are old. For one reason or another, some of the books that had information on this subject seemed to have been removed from my local county courthouse. I recommend that you visit the county courthouse law library. If you have read this far, even if you decide not to change your status you will probably find it very interesting.

If you have a computer and a modem you can connect up to bulletin boards that are dedicated to the sovereignty issue. A very good bulletin board is located in California. The telephone number is 1-818-888-9882 and the line attributes are BAUD rate up to 14.4, Parity - none, Data bits - 8, Stop bits - 1. If you do not live in the 818 area code, it will cost you the toll charges. There is no charge for using the board. There is a file on there that contains the telephone numbers of other bulletin boards. Perhaps you can find a number with your area code so you can avoid the toll charges. The bulletin board has files pertaining to two subjects. The first is restoring the rights that you lost when you lost your state Citizenship. The second is trying to prevent the loss of more rights by opposing the New World Order, that is losing your US citizenship status to become a UN citizen. A word of warning must be given at this point. Some of the people who do basic legal research start out with some extremely unusual conspiracy theories that they try to prove. You may be offended at these theories. Time will tell if the conspiracies exist or not. Dispite this the research is very valuable.

ANTISHYSTER is a paper that is published six times a year. It is "A CRITICAL EXAMINATION OF THE AMERICAN LEGAL SYSTEM." This excellent publication is about 60 pages. The annual subscription is $25.00 but, if you order as a group (3 subscriptions or more at the same time) it is only $15.00. This is money well spent. You can reach them at (214) 418-8993 or send cash, check, or money order to: AntiShyster c/o P.O.B. 540786 Dallas, Texas 75354-0786. You can order by Visa or Master Card at (800) 477-5508.

The AMERICAN'S BULLETIN is a monthly newspaper that is dedicated to be "A VOICE OF OPPOSITION TO TYRANNY". It is printed in Oregon and is mailed across the nation. Accept for a few articles about unconventional ideas on alternative health care the newspaper seems to be exclusively dedicated to Citizenship. You can call them at 1-503-779-7709. The cost is $25.00 a year. You can get it shipped without a ZIP Code but it cost $30.00 because it will be shipped via first class mail. There are advanced topics that I have not described in this paper printed every month.

PERCEPTIONS is a magazine that is published four times a year. It has articles about Citizenship but it also has articles UFOs, Astrology, and alternative health strategies. The cost is $15.00 a year. You can reach them at: Perceptions, 11664 National Blvd., No. 314, Los Angeles, California 90064.

THE SPOTLIGHT is a newspaper that reports on the New World Order and how it is being implemented. You can reach them at 300 Independence Ave. SE, Washington, D.C. 20003.

The LA Lawman is a television show that is broadcast on cable TV in California. You can by a copy of the 30 minute videotapes on issues relating to state Citizens and perhaps even get them broadcast in your area. You can reach The LA Lawman at 9245 Reseda Blvd Suite 450 Northridge CA 91324 or at (818) 366-6187.

There are many good books that you may want. LEGAL RESEARCH - How To Find and Understand the Law by attorneys Stephen Elias & Susan Levinkind is a good introduction to the law library. It is published by Nolo Press in 1992. It costs $16.95. Before getting this book, I was never in a law library but now, I can do legal research!

The FEDERALIST PAPERS by Alexander Hamilton, James Madison, & John Jay is published by Mentor. The paperback cost $5.99. This book can be downloaded from the bulletin board listed above. It contains more than 500 pages of arguments that Hamilton, Madison, and Jay wrote to be published in the local papers for the purpose of ratifying the Constitution. The Supreme Court sometimes quotes the Federalist Papers in its decisions. If you want to know what the Constitution means, then this is the book for you.

THE ANTI-FEDERALIST by the Opponents if the Constitution is published by The University of Chicago Press. The articles in this book were published in the local papers for the purpose of not ratifying the Constitution. It is not quite as good as the Federalist Papers but, it also determines what the framers of the constitution were thinking.

LIBERTY LIBRARY publishes a booklet that contains the Declaration of Independence, US Constitution, Bill of Rights, and a description of jurors rights. A single copy is $1.50; but if you buy 20 or more, the cost is only $0.50 a piece. I find it amazing that all through public school, I never read more than two paragraphs from any of these documents. Every child should have the opportunity to have a copy of this booklet. You can reach Liberty Library at 300 Independence Ave., SE, Washington, D.C. 20003.

DEMOCRACY IN AMERICA by Alexis De Tocqueville is published by Anchor Books (DOUBLEDAY & COMPANY, INC.) De Tocqueville traveled around the United States of America in the 1830s & 1840s. He compared, in minute detail, the differences between how the American Republics were run and how the French Republic was run. If you want to see how the nation existed without income taxes and government bureaucracies, then this is the book for you. It is kind of long (almost 800 pages).

The Federal Zone by Mitch Modeleski can be downloaded from the bulletin board listed above. It describes in more detail how the federal government usurped power of the states by creating a federal zone that nearly swallowed the states. The IRS code is explained.

Invisible Contracts by George Mercier can be downloaded from the bulletin board listed above. This book describes the adhesion contracts that bind people into federal jurisdiction. It also about conspiracies by the New World Order people. It is written from the perspective of a Mormon. Mormon religious ideas are described in great detail and with great fervor. The information on adhesion contracts is very enlightening. Please note that the bulletin boards and phone numbers listed above do change often, as I'm sure you can imagine the hate trolls that often scower the boards, but with a few clicks in today's world, they shouldn't be hard to locate.

CONCLUSION

The ideas in this book may be new to you. You may not believe them. You may like the federal system. If you have read this far, I hope you will see the government in a different light.

Let's restate the central premise of this book.

The government recognizes two distinct classes of citizens: a state Citizen and a federal citizen. Each has different rights and responsibilities. State Citizens created the states who created the federal government who created federal citizens. Most people are born state Citizens and become federal citizens without their knowledge sometime after birth. You can reclaim your state Citizenship status through a legal procedure. If you remain a federal citizen, you will pay lots of taxes and have no rights. If you reclaim your state Citizenship status, you will have to learn about our legal system and you will have to change the way you bank, and save, and invest, and other aspects of modern living that probably taken for granted. But a state Citizen that knows the legal system has more control over his/her life. Information is power. For decades the information, and the power, has been centralized by the government class. Today, the balance of power is shifting. As Citizens become more vigilant about government encroachments, the government's power is lessened. As the number of state Citizens mushrooms, you will hear about them in the press as the empire strikes back. This movement is not trying to change the system -- this is the way it works now! In fact, any attempt to change the Constitution via a constitutional convention or international treaty should be opposed strongly. Can you imagine what sort of constitution would be written if our current political leaders do the writing? Now you know what this movement is all about. Whether you decide to change your status is up to you.

Please send a copy of this book to everybody that you think is smart enough to understand it.

www.ingramcontent.com/pod-product-compliance
Lightning Source LLC
Chambersburg PA
CBHW031505210526
45463CB00003B/1093